S

Surviving On Broken Pieces

By Gina Johnson

Gina Johnson

Surviving On Broken Pieces

Gina Johnson

Surviving On Broken Pieces

Surviving On Broken Pieces, Copyright 2015 by Gina Johnson. All Rights reserved. Printed in the United States of America. No part of this book may be used or reproduced in any manner whatsoever without written permission except in the case of brief quotations embodied in critical articles and reviews. For information, contact Tenacious Books, 9701 Wilshire Blvd, 10th floor, Beverly Hills, CA 90212. (888) 501-4448.

1st Edition—copyright 2015

Johnson, Gina, *Surviving On Broken Pieces*, 1st ed.

ISBN

Tenacious Books, Publisher

9701 Wilshire Blvd.

10th floor

Beverly Hills, CA 90212

Gina Johnson

Surviving On Broken Pieces

Surviving On Broken Pieces

By Gina Johnson

Gina Johnson

Surviving On Broken Pieces

Dedication

I dedicate this book to the young marriage class of the Portland Street COGIC, better known as the Bishop Goodwin Memorial Cathedral. Thank you for allowing me to teach. I love you and will never forget the times we had together. No matter where life takes me, I will never forget you.

Gina Johnson

Surviving On Broken Pieces

Special Thanks

To my parents, Bishop RD Edward and Mother Dollie Goodwin, who stood by me through all of my tests and trials, and prayed for me. They knew what it meant for me to walk in faith.

To my sister, Denise Williams-Wilson, whom I love dearly, who tried hard not to allow her love for me to get in the way of God's plan in my life.

To my brother Reuben, who always encouraged me and helped me with my struggles as I faced them. And who saw enough in my writing to make sure that this book was published. He believed in me and in my story. I got divorced in 2002 and he stayed with me during the process of writing the book and finally, getting me through the process of getting the book published. No words of love or gratitude are strong enough to express what I feel for him.

To Reuben's wife, Kim, who was a part of my young married women's class and encouraged me to keep the devil from stopping me.

To my brother, Pastor Edward Goodwin, Jr., who had enough faith in me that he trusted me with the young married women of his church. He believed that I could pass the ultimate test. To his wife Chandra, who never gave up on me and stuck close to my side through it all.

To my children Jerlina and Dominique, who I love with all my heart. They have given me their love and encouragement no matter what.

To my prayer partner, Miss Toni, who did not understand my position all the time, but kept going to pray with me.

And to my goddaughter Angel, who has given her undying love to me, making possible everything that I ever asked of her. Thank you so much—Godmommy loves you.

Gina Johnson

Surviving On Broken Pieces

Finally, thank you to Pastor Hutton, who delivered the inspiring sermon that prompted me to tell my story of surviving on broken pieces.

Gina Goodwin Johnson

Surviving On Broken Pieces

Chapter One—Life Growing Up

"When we are children we seldom think of the future. This innocence leaves us free to enjoy ourselves as few adults can. The day we fret about the future is the day we leave our childhood behind." — Patrick Rothfuss

You know how people have to look back and analyze their lives in order to determine whether or not they had a good childhood? Well, that's not the case for me. I enjoyed every bit of my childhood.

Surviving On Broken Pieces

I was happy to be a child and enjoy the good life. I didn't have a lot of responsibilities. In fact, the biggest responsibility was focusing on school and church—everything else was gravy.

It wasn't like today where children can't really be children because they have to grow up too quickly. I look around now and I see children having children and mothers not mothering the children they have.

I was born in 1963 in Harvey, Illinois, a relatively small south suburban town, twenty miles from Chicago.

Gina Johnson

Surviving On Broken Pieces

My parents--Bishop Edward and Dollie Goodwin—strong believers of the word of God, took a particular liking to certain scriptures in the Bible and those scriptures governed our lives. You know, the scriptures, that when quoted, generally meant that rules of conduct had been breached and the penalty was severe. Proverbs 22:6: "Train up a child in the way that he should go and when he is old he will not depart from it."

I felt that my parents should have known that whatever it was that I was being accused of, I didn't do and that the punishment should have gone to one of the boys in the house. But my parents, even in punishment, were always very loving, and I knew that even while being punished for training purposes, I was still loved.

I remember playing outside with my friends and walking to Dixie Square, the big Harvey mall at the time. It had all kinds of stores under one roof. There were wig shops, barber shops, perfume shops, eateries and all the major department stores. On occasion, we would get permission from our parents to go to the mall while the boys were getting haircuts. The style for men was the "Blowout."

Gina Johnson

Surviving On Broken Pieces

We had fun at the mall until in closed down. We were very disappointed, but it was hard for the stores to make money when some people decided that it was better to steal than to pay for the merchandise.

It wasn't that people wanted the mall to close. In fact, most people complained that it closed and expressed that they didn't understand why black people couldn't keep a mall in the 'hood. The theft took a huge toll on the business owners and they didn't have security devices to catch people in the act.

When things started getting rough at the mall, my parents stopped letting us go

Surviving On Broken Pieces

alone. The only time we went was when my brothers were getting haircuts or to shop for Easter and Christmas at Sears.

Harvey is a small town and at the time of my childhood, the only significance the town had for me, was that my family and friends lived there. I had no idea that the town wasn't highly ranked socially or that it was any different from any other small town.

We would have the occasional break in, but even that seemed okay, because Daddy would just chase the burglar away, pray and we would all go to bed. I can't say that I wasn't scared at times, but Dad was always home at night and he always prayed with us and that made things a lot easier to deal with. My siblings and I grew very close, primarily because we were forced to be each other's best friends growing up. We were almost never allowed out of the yard without adult supervision and even more rarely allowed off the block. At times, I felt that we were prisoners of "Honore," which was the block we lived on. The fact that we had so much together time has proven to be beneficial as adults.

There was one family in particular that my family grew close to during our Harvey experience. They were a married couple with children close to our ages.

Surviving On Broken Pieces

Our parents got to know each other and soon, their mother joined our church and that made the children instant friends. We could spend time with each other in the backyards!

It was great having a couple of new friends that we could spend time with, talking and laughing. We could share our church experiences without getting laughed at for being church kids. We grew close and got creative in our backyard experiences, which still make me laugh nearly thirty years later.

My family lived in what was really a two bedroom house with a living room, dining room, kitchen, den and basement.
Gina Johnson

Surviving On Broken Pieces

Dad took the den area and made it into a bedroom for the boys and my sister and I slept in the room across from our parents. The house was all brick with a wonderful fireplace in the living room. When there was no church, we would spend winter evenings roasting marshmallows and talking as a family.

We never ever felt poor, but there were signs that things were sometimes tight.

We shared a lot of things. For example, my youngest brother would get hand-me-downs when my older brother would grow out of pants and shirts. We ate a lot of beans and soups. My father is still a master at making soups, to the point where the whole family will still race to his house when Mom tips us off that he's made a pot of soup!

I remember winter days when Dad would catch the snow fresh as it fell from the sky and make ice cream out of it. I guess that should have been a cue that we didn't have everything, but we thought it was fun.

My parents would host holiday parties for their "saved" friends and family. I recall them playing ping-pong and hours of Scrabble. Scrabble was the game that was played at every family function and without question, gave bragging rights to the winner until the next holiday gathering. Dad and Mom would play and I would be so proud when one of them would have won the most games in that day.

I remember one couple that stood out from anyone else mainly because they were not just occasional visitors on specific holidays. They lived in Waukegan, Illinois, which is two and a half hours north of Harvey. My family would also drive to their home to spend time with them, in addition to the times they would come to our home. We would go on trips together to the Wisconsin Dells and stay in cabins and watch water shows. It was great because everyone got along just fine. We had some other kids to play with, talk to and get in trouble with. We spent so much time together that my parents didn't object to us calling the adults "uncle" and "aunt" and the children "cousin."

It was the combination of these events that set my ideas, expectations and values for "family." These events represented a piece of ideology or memory burned into my brain the way a certain familiar scent can remind you of your grandmother's cooking when you were a child.

These memories were puzzle pieces so masterfully connected that they show a picture of beautiful family togetherness—a whole family together—the laughter and the suffering all included. It meant that love had to work one way or another.

My siblings and I were very close and we made things work one way or another.

We would sit around and try to figure out ways to make money. We had a friend who was like a brother who would work with us to figure out what we could do to make money while our parents were gone.

The reason we needed money was to be able to buy candy, cookies, gum and pop.

Gina Johnson

Surviving On Broken Pieces

If you had enough sweets, no one could ruin your day.

One day, while we were brainstorming, we came up with the idea of having a carnival. With this great idea, we could make money and have fun at the same time. Our parents would be gone for a while, so we decided to have the carnival in our backyard.

We spent the whole day planning and making hand written flyers. My brothers and our friend passed the flyers out all over the neighborhood. We figured that maybe a handful of people would come out to see what was going on—mostly out of curiosity since no one had really

Surviving On Broken Pieces

heard of having a carnival in a backyard. Instead of a handful of people showing up, kids from all over Harvey came.

I loved carnivals and can still remember the cotton candy and the smell of hot dogs, hamburgers, elephant ears and corndogs. I guess a lot of people enjoyed carnivals as much as we did.

The carnival rides included a high flying swing made from a few jump ropes and an old board left over from some work Dad had finished around the house. We drilled holes in the wood and tied the rope to the wood as tight as we could. My youngest brother and his friend climbed the tree and hung the rope and the high flying swing was ready to go.

We had games that we made from boards and anything we could find around the house and garage. We made the rules up as we went along, so very few people won those games. No one really cared, because they had so much fun on the swing and the games for the low price of ten cents.

Our feature attraction, however, was "Sally Boo," a black 1967 Ford stick shift car. "Old Sally Boo" was what Dad named her, and we were glad to have her!

Surviving On Broken Pieces

If you wanted to take a ride on Sally Boo, you had to pay and pay big! It cost fifty cents per person per ride and we had a line that was forever long. While people lined up, my sister collected the money. Kids would get in the car and we would show them how to put it in neutral. Once in neutral, the boys would push the car while the passenger would steer. They would push it out of the driveway into the street and back into the yard again.

As we made money, I would run to the store and buy candy to share with everyone.

We were making big bucks and having the time of our lives doing it--so much so that we didn't notice the time passing so quickly.

We had the car in the street just as had many times, but this time was different because we could see Mom and Dad's car quickly approaching the house. Everyone was trying to help push the car back into the driveway to her rightful place, but we were dead meat and we knew it.

Trouble is a mild word for what happened to us.

Later, after getting into big trouble, we sat down to discuss the proceeds of our carnival. Their thinking was that at least we got some money out of it, but I had to inform them that we had actually spent all of the money on candy. Not only did we get in trouble, but we were broke again. On the bright side, at least we had a lot of fun.

We always found ways to have fun. Even my childhood experiences at church were filled with fun.

Not going to church wasn't an option, so we made the best of it. We loved going to church and even visiting other churches to meet other young people. We even loved church musicals.

The church was our social life, really, and if one young person got in trouble, it usually resulted in all the young people getting in trouble. We had dedicated youth leaders and most of the ties that were established back then in the church have proven to be lifelong ties.

My parents worked hard to give us the best education they could. The four of us attended private school all the way until high school. My oldest sister even spent a few years at a private high school.

Private school wasn't all that great and was particularly hard on some of us than on others. Our school only had eight black people and four of them were family members.

Gina Johnson

Surviving On Broken Pieces

We got into trouble a lot because we were rebellious. This was the seventies and so much was going on around black rights while we were in a majority (90%) white school.

I remember going through a period where I wished I wasn't a Goodwin.

I felt that it was wrong and too much pressure to be in my family because I couldn't do many of the things that everyone else was doing because I had to be a good example for others to follow.

People were quick to threaten to tell my parents if I got out of line.

Gina Johnson

Surviving On Broken Pieces

Back then if an adult say you did something, you did it—regardless as to whether or not you actually had. If you smarted off, you would get in trouble by the adult who caught you and by your parents when you got home.

Those were the rules and everyone knew them.

I had to find myself and realize that I was blessed to have a family to love me.

I am who I am for a purpose, because not everyone is blessed to come from a good Christian home with love.

My father didn't run the streets, he stayed at home with us and provided love, food, comfort and a roof over our heads. He and my Mom prayed over us and raised us together.

I appreciate who I am and I appreciate the sacrifices my parents made so that I could become the woman I am today. I take my hat off to them for the long talks and not allowing young men to take advantage of me. They helped me to value saving myself for my husband and taught me how to be a wife and a lady.

I look back today and I appreciate every whipping, every punishment, every scripture they read over me and all the time we spent in church as a family.

Gina Johnson

Surviving On Broken Pieces

Gina Johnson

Chapter Two—Family Ties

"The family: We were a strange little band of characters trudging through life sharing diseases and toothpaste, coveting one another's desserts, hiding shampoo, borrowing money, locking each other out of our rooms, inflicting pain and kissing to heal it in the same instant, loving, laughing, defending, and trying to figure out the common thread that bound us all together."
-- Erma Bombeck

Sometimes, I sit and wonder whether it was my sister leaving me to get married while I was so young that caused me to end up being spoiled. Maybe it's because

Surviving On Broken Pieces

I have always had my father and two brothers to look after me and take up for me. Whatever the case, I can appreciate the extra attention that I received in life from my family.

I remember feeling so alone the day my sister got married. I was so angry with her for leaving me. She had always protected me and I didn't know what I was going to do. I would be starting high school and she would be gone. It made me angry and afraid.

I even recall my sister taking up for me to the point where she told my mother to give her a whipping instead of me!

Gina Johnson

Surviving On Broken Pieces

Well, we both ended up getting the beat down.

I felt spoiled, and maybe it's because I have always been a daddy's girl. Or maybe all of my parents' children were spoiled in different ways.

At thirteen, I was still knocking on my parents' door, telling them I was scared, which meant that I was coming in and I wanted them to move over and make room for me.

My mother sheltered me, which really meant that I was never going to spend the night with anyone other than my grandparents. I can appreciate it now,

Surviving On Broken Pieces

because there are so many horror stories about bad things that happened to children while in the care of people the family trusted.

I remember falling asleep at church at twelve, and instead of my father waking me up, he carried me to the car.

My grandfather, "Papa," played a very important part in my life. He was a great grandparent to me. There was nothing he wouldn't do for me. I could talk to him about almost anything because I was his baby. I miss him very much. I remember getting the call to come to the hospital and say my final farewell to him. I cried for days, weeks, maybe months. In fact, I think about him sometimes now and tears come to my eyes.

My grandmother, "Dear" would always talk to me as a child and tell me how to treat my husband, if I ever got one. I thought that since I was just a girl, she shouldn't have been telling me those things. Of course, I can appreciate those things now, even though, to some people, they seem to be old fashioned values with no place in these modern times.

One of the things that she would say to me had to do with living with an unsaved husband. She taught me that just because

Surviving On Broken Pieces

a husband is not saved doesn't mean that he's not the man of the house. It doesn't mean that the two people can't live together and have peace. I wish she was still here so I could ask her what to do when you've done everything and still can't get your husband to live with you. One of her most famous quotes was: "You can't use this now, but put it on the shelf. You will need it later."

My other grandmother, Suge, also played a great part in my life. She helped my parents raise us.

I remember as a young girl, she would sit and talk to me and tell me what it meant to have a family. She said to never let

Surviving On Broken Pieces

anyone come between me and my siblings. She said we should protect each other and never go to bed angry—we could argue, but never throw a punch.

She did what she could to take care of us. There were no limits. She would always tell me that I would miss her when she was gone and I think about her often because I really do miss her.

But I had two very protective brothers who acted like their jobs were to ruin my life.

I was the baby of the family, even though my brother Reuben was younger than me. He was a protector, so it was like he was a big brother to me.

I remember going on my first date. It was a big event in my house. It was like going on the prom—which was not an option in our house—you didn't even think about asking to go because my father followed the word of the Lord and our pastor said it was wrong to go, so we weren't going.

But I could go on a date if my brothers would tag along and I was excited. I was already eighteen, but, that's how things went in our home.

Surviving On Broken Pieces

The young man came over to the house and talked to my parents while I got ready. We went to a restaurant and my brothers and their friend followed us and sat in the restaurant.

I can honestly say that I enjoyed high school. I was saved and some of the guys considered me to be stuck up, but they still each tried to be the one that got me. Some of them were nice, but my Dad taught me that there is no good devil and I believed in his words.

When I started dating, my Dad would have long Daddy talks with me. He taught me that if a young man felt I owed him something because he paid for

Surviving On Broken Pieces

dinner, then I should pay him back for dinner. I could just come to Daddy and he would give me the money. He gave me a sense of self-respect that lasted through my teen years.

My daddy would always tell me that he was depending on me to live for God and make a stand no matter what all the other girls were doing. He trusted me and no matter what I faced in life, it meant the world to me that he trusted me. I always did my best not to make him ashamed of me.

Even when my mother would suggest that I not go somewhere, my daddy would let me go and tell my mother that he trusted me. Not that my mother didn't trust me—she just didn't have as much faith in me as my father did.

My mother put a lot into me. She taught me how to keep myself together as a woman. She taught me how to keep my house clean and take care of children and to be the best wife I could be, even through marriage issues. She would tell me to never let my husband leave the house hungry and to always take care of his sexual needs. There was never any room to be tired or have a headache.

I learned a lot from my family and I loved family gatherings.

Gina Johnson

Surviving On Broken Pieces

Family dinners were great!

All of the families would come together on holidays to eat. I remember my uncles playing with us and allowing us to be children. My Aunties would make sure that all of the cousins knew each other by name and would tell us to look after each other.

Now that we are grown up we can still depend on each other if needed.

Christmas was my favorite holiday. I would go to bed on Christmas Eve so excited about the next day that I could hardly sleep. My parents would hang our stockings over the fireplace and I could smell the fresh apples and oranges that hung in the stockings.

I'm not sure if every parent used actual socks for Christmas stockings but it became a thing of tradition in our house to use Dad's "clean" socks for stockings. We would treat those socks like they were good stockings from Walgreen's. Even when my parents got to a place financially where they could afford to go and buy Christmas Stockings from a store, we still used Daddy's socks. I laugh when I think about it, because the socks would stretch all the way out because of the weight of the apples, oranges, nuts and candy.

Gina Johnson

Surviving On Broken Pieces

Christmas tradition centered around our religious beliefs. We never celebrated the season without remembering the reason first. We went to church at six in the morning for Sunrise Service, which was on Easter and Thanksgiving as well.

In the church, all the children had to behave. If one child got in trouble, we would all be in trouble. We didn't play in church. My father could give us one look and we knew there was trouble. He never promised a whipping without delivering—he said he didn't want to disappoint us. My mother would sometimes forget, but when she would remember, you would beg the Lord for mercy. Today, it might be considered child abuse, but I never felt abused. I knew my parents loved us and the discipline kept us out of jail and made us respect our elders.

We got up early and after getting dressed for church, we were allowed to open one gift, but only if we were dressed on time. My dad believed that we should give God praise before opening all the gifts. My two brothers would always get up and get dressed on time and then rush my sister and I. sometimes we made it and sometimes we didn't. Then we piled in the car to go to church. When we returned home, we could open the rest

Surviving On Broken Pieces

of the gifts and play before going to celebrate Christmas with the rest of the family.

We would typically go over to Papa's house and meet up with our cousins, uncles and aunts.

Gifts from certain relatives were predictable because we received the same type of gift every year, like books or memory bible games. But every year we would go, wishing that one certain uncle would be there, because he gave great presents. Sometimes he would be there, and other times he would show up a little later that year or early the next year with our gifts still wrapped up in

Surviving On Broken Pieces

Christmas paper. But no matter when he gave them to us, we were never disappointed.

Childhood was great. Sometimes, I wish I could go back to the years when I was free of problems. I just depended on Daddy and Momma.

Life can sure take you for a ride.

Surviving On Broken Pieces

Gina Johnson

Surviving On Broken Pieces

Chapter Three—I Do

"Love is patient and kind; love does not envy or boast; it is not arrogant or rude. It does not insist on its own way; it is not irritable or resentful; it does not rejoice at wrongdoing, but rejoices with the truth. Love bears all things, believes all things, hopes all things, endures all things." 1st Corinthians

I met my husband on a Sunday night in Chicago at a gas station.

It was 1986, and he was pumping gas while I was acting silly with my sister and a close friend.

Surviving On Broken Pieces

His name was Jerrold and he came over and gave me his number. I gave him my sister's number. He called me for one week straight and I didn't return his call until my sister prodded me to. After she chastised me, I went in her room and called him back.

Jerrold and I spoke to each other on the phone for an entire month before we saw each other again. He asked me to attend a musical at his church, so I went and took a friend with me.

I had only seen him one time, so naturally, I had forgotten what he looked like. The friend who was with me at the musical was a different friend from the one who was at the gas station when Jerrold and I met, so she wasn't much help. I kept pointing to different guys, but neither of them was Jerrold.

Finally, church had ended and Jerrold approached me. He asked if I was Gina and I said yes.

We had a whirlwind romance. From the moment we saw each other at the church musical, we began to talk every day. We began to date frequently and within one year, we were getting married.

We got married inside of a year because Jerrold was really into me. he went above and beyond to show me that he was dedicated to me.

Jerrold was at church more than I was, because he would go to his own church and then come to my church. He would get off work and go home to get his car and then drive thirty miles to come and see me.

But just before the wedding, I was given some news that I thought would rock our very foundation.

Jerrold's best friend called and said he wanted to talk to me about a problem his friend was having. He said his friend was younger than the woman he was dating, but the woman didn't know. He asked me what I would do if I found out that the man I was dating had lied to me. I told him that I would break up over the lie.

He said thanks and hung up. About five minutes later, Jerrold called and admitted that his best friend was referring to him. He told me that he was only nineteen and I freaked out.

I didn't realize that it was Jerrold who was lying. We had already discussed age and I thought that we were both the same age.

Gina Johnson

Surviving On Broken Pieces

He said that he had to admit it before the marriage because his mother told him that you're not supposed to start a marriage with a lie.

I didn't talk to him for a week. I was trying to figure out what to do. I just wanted to run away.

My mother kept telling me that he had called, but I didn't want to talk to him. The wedding was getting closer, but I really unhappy with the information I had received. I still wanted time to process it.

Finally, my mother came in my room to talk to me. She said that someone was getting married after all the money they had spent, so it may as well be me. She pointed out the fact that we would still be able to grow old together.

I was still very upset, but my feelings were involved. I still loved him.

I decided to leave it up to God. I had told myself that I would never marry anyone younger than me, so I wondered if this was against God. I wished for someone else to tell me what to do. I prayed for God to let my father or grandfather know. When I asked them, they said God didn't tell them anything.

Gina Johnson

Surviving On Broken Pieces

I decided that without any intervention from God, I would have to go ahead with the wedding.

Once I made that decision, I began to get the wedding plans together and I was very excited.

The day came and it was my turn to say: "I do."

I was scared, but Jerrold had made feel so secure and loved, that I knew this was my dream come true.

On May 23, 1987, I said "I do," and it was one of the happiest days of my life. The wedding was like no other—like a dream

Surviving On Broken Pieces

come true. Everything I thought I wanted in my wedding, I had.

My parents were so very proud of me. I was twenty-three and I was still a virgin.

I felt like I was in a dream world. Nothing could go wrong, because I was marrying my prince. Jerrold loved me and he was saved. He had God and that was more important than anything. He had grown up in the church just like me. Life was going to be great.

The day of the wedding was very exciting.

I was about three hours late because I was very nervous. I wasn't hesitant to get

Surviving On Broken Pieces

married, I was just hesitant to go through the actual wedding and I have no idea why. The wedding was supposed to start at three o'clock and at five o'clock I finally told my driver that I was ready

The church was forty minutes away. I was certain that everyone had left, including Jerrold, but, in fact, the church was packed when I arrived.

Jerrold asked me later why I was so late. He said that he was worried that I wouldn't show. I told him that it was just nerves.

There were about fifty people involved in the wedding. By the time the songs

Surviving On Broken Pieces

had been sung and the wedding party went down the aisle, I was ready. I told my dad that I loved him and he told me that he was proud of me. He also said that if I didn't want to do it, he would tell everyone to leave.

I wanted to go through it, so I told him that I was ready.

When the church doors opened, I could see that all eight hundred and fifty seats were filled. It scared me to death.

I began the long walk down the aisle and all I could do was pray to God for strength. I prayed that I was doing the right thing and that Jerrold was the right man.

While Jerrold and I had the one small problem over age, I really trusted that we were good for each other and that life would be great. I believed that Jerrold would take care of me and that we would work together to have a great life with each other.

I didn't have a clue about life.

People would try to warn me about some of the difficulties that people face in marriage, but I wouldn't listen. I thought that nothing could ever come between us. I put my husband on such a high pedestal that it would make people mad. People would try to tell me that I viewed Jerrold like God. I didn't think of him as God, but I loved him very much.

I would ask myself why people were unable to see Jerrold the way I saw him—the perfect man for me, filled with goodness. He was one of the greatest men I knew. I had left my daddy's home to be with a man who loved me just as much. What could possibly go wrong?

I was Daddy's little spoiled brat and life was just beginning to teach me its lessons.

Surviving On Broken Pieces

One of those lessons was in the form of my soon to be husband.

Jerrold had street knowledge and I only had church knowledge. What does that equal? Issues!

I'm not saying that marriage wasn't wonderful, because it was—especially when it was new. I was in Gina's own little dreamland. But I thought that marriage was forever without a lot of issues and that's just not how life works.

How could I have been so naïve?

Jerrold and I loved each other, but there were things that just didn't make sense. Things that would come between us and turn our dream life into a nightmare. Some of it was his fault and some of it was mine.

For example, when we had been married for a while, Jerrold told me that I was selfish. It would make me so angry to hear that, because I didn't view myself that way. I would ask him why he thought that, but I would never get a straight answer.

I went to the mall one day and came back with bags of things that I had bought for myself. I had a pair of socks for him. He went ballistic!

Surviving On Broken Pieces

He kept talking about how beautiful it was that I thought of him. He said it was nice that I bought something for my husband—the husband who gives me whatever pleases me.

He was being sarcastic. When I realized the message he was delivering with sarcasm, it hit me. it hit me hard.

From that point, I never went to the store without remembering my husband. I might pick up his favorite ice cream or his favorite candy, but I would always do something to show that I appreciated him.

Gina Johnson

Surviving On Broken Pieces

And there were other issues that he had with me.

Jerrold began to complain that I was putting my family ahead of him.

I am a family girl and my family and I are very close. We were just raised that way. My grandmother was very persistent with assuring that we all look out for each other.

My husband liked my family and I liked his. I had no little sisters and he had two that I took as my own. Our families even got along well with each other.

It all seemed so perfect.

Gina Johnson

Surviving On Broken Pieces

I didn't understand what he meant when he said that I was putting my family before him. It's not like my family was at our house every day. I would talk to them every day, but that was to make sure they were okay. And, we didn't even see all of them at church. Two of my siblings aren't even saved, so they never went to church.

I had a "whatever" attitude, because I knew my husband loved me, so I didn't think it was a real issue. I thought that all we needed was love.

At this point, I would say to other women that yes, love is important, but since we live in this world where there is more than just love, you also need to

Surviving On Broken Pieces

listen to what your man is trying to tell you. Don't block out what your man is trying to tell you under any circumstances.

My husband was reaching out to me and I didn't even realize it.

And life began to get more complicated.

I found out that I was pregnant with my first child.

When Jerrold got the news, he began to love me even more. He treated me like a queen.

Surviving On Broken Pieces

I was having his parents' first grandchild and my husband was becoming a proud father. He was with me all the way.

The day I was delivering, my parents' car was in the shop, so they were using ours to get to church. At about 11pm, I was feeling a little uneasy. Jerrold jumped up, called my dad and grabbed my bags.

In no time, my dad was at my house, but I wanted to know where my mother was. My dad said there was no time to wait, so we left for the hospital, which was about ten miles away. By the time we arrived, my mother was walking through the door of the hospital. She had convinced my oldest brother to bring her.

Gina Johnson

Surviving On Broken Pieces

I was in labor for twenty-eight hours and it was an experience that I can't even explain.

My husband didn't leave my side. He was in the delivery room the whole time. He was so happy to be having a child. He was my heart and I loved him, but I vowed right then and there that I would not be going through this experience again.

I was fine with one child, but my husband had other plans for me.

Three and a half years later, I was having a second baby—another daughter. My husband and I had a heart to heart talk and we decided together that this would be the extent of our family. I knew he wanted to try again to have a son, but I felt that if God wanted us to have a son, we would have had one already. We talked about the possibility of adopting a boy, but that conversation never went anywhere.

My husband was a good father and helped me a great deal with the girls. He was very protective of them. He changed diapers and bottles and we would take turns getting up at night when they needed us.

But we began to have issues by the time the second baby was three months old.

Gina Johnson

Surviving On Broken Pieces

My husband left me twice and I was in a mental state that I had never been in before. I had lost so much weight that I was down to a size three.

People began talking.

My parents and the rest of my family were very concerned for me. I remember thinking that this is not the way my life was supposed to be. I prayed to God and asked why I wasn't happy. I knew I hadn't lived a perfect life, but I wasn't bad, either.

I took a mental list of myself: I kept the children clean and I kept a very clean house. I cooked a minimum of three days a week. And, I never denied sex to my husband—no matter what (I was taught by my mom that a wife never allows a man to have an excuse to cheat on you).

But something was wrong, because my husband had left me.

And I became angry, even turning my anger towards God.

My father came over one Sunday and told my mother to come in and help the children get dressed while I got ready for church. He talked to me like a woman. He told me that God hadn't done anything to me. He said that as humans, we forget that God loves us and would never do anything to destroy us or hurt us. He simply allows us to prove our love to him.

I went to church that day and declared that the devil would not have my marriage.

My husband came back home.

I thought the difficulty was all over.

But the devil was not finished with me. He was simply allowing me to have a breather.

The Lord knows how much we can take, but I had no idea.

Gina Johnson

Surviving On Broken Pieces

Gina Johnson

Chapter Four: Following Love

"What you won't do, you do for love, you've tried everything, but you won't give up. In my world, only you, make me do for love, what I would not do..."--from "What You Won't do For Love," by Bobby Caldwell.

Some of us will go to extreme limits to keep the love we have.

For me, I moved halfway across the nation, with my little girls in tow, to try to keep the man that I loved.

In my heart, I truly believed that I could keep together what God had joined.

Gina Johnson

Surviving On Broken Pieces

But what happens when you realize that God didn't put a thing together?

I truly thought that God had put Jerrold and I together. And based on that thought, I wanted to pray us into marital bliss. I wanted to pray us through our difficulties so that we could live together with the love that God had intended for us to have.

But I began to question myself. Did I think that my husband was perfect? Did love have me so blind that I couldn't see him for who he really was?

What began to come into my thoughts was the reality that God may not have

Surviving On Broken Pieces

put us together. Perhaps we did that ourselves and perhaps God was actually trying to release me, but I was fighting. I thought I was fighting to save what God had created, but perhaps I was actually fighting what God actually wanted for me.

What happens when you are living in a marriage where you are more alone than if you were single? What happens when people look at you and think you have the perfect life?

I had a lot of questions in my head. But I really thought the one answer was to keep holding on to my love and to do anything to keep our love intact.
Gina Johnson

Surviving On Broken Pieces

I had been married now for about seven years and my perfect world had started crumbling. Things began to change drastically and quickly. Things that were once okay were no longer okay. Where my husband was once happy, he didn't seem to be happy anymore.

It seemed that in order for him to regain his happiness, he needed to do something radically different. He needed to shake things up. And he needed me to follow his plan as his wife.

After ten years of marriage, my husband came to me and said that he wanted to move away from everything we had grown up around and everything we had built.

Initially, I was resistant. In fact, I refused to even consider it. As a result, he left me. Again.

Jerrold and I had a six month old baby and a four year old baby, and he left me because he wasn't happy. He left me because I didn't want the same thing he wanted.

I was devastated when he left. He had left before, but it still hurt. And it still felt like I was being torn to pieces.

Surviving On Broken Pieces

My perfect dream world was falling apart. Again. I couldn't sleep or function correctly.

I tried to hold my ground because I really didn't want to move. But I really didn't want to lose my husband.

Three weeks later, I agreed to move away. I made the decision because I sincerely thought it would save my marriage and I was committed to succeeding with Jerrold.

Jerrold wanted to move to Denver, Colorado. I had prayed that he would change his mind, but he had already begun making plans as soon as I had agreed. I pleaded with him and talked about how our children's extended families would be left behind. His response was that he was our family.

The plan was that we would get rid of our home and while he went to Denver to get things set up, I would stay at my parents' home with the children.

Things moved quickly and before I knew it, he was in Denver.

He stayed with some of my family in Denver while he looked for a job.

He loved Denver. He wanted us there and I assumed that he loved us as much as he loved the new atmosphere.

Gina Johnson

Surviving On Broken Pieces

I assumed it, because after he was there for a month, he kept calling me telling me how much he missed me and how he missed the children. He said that he really needed me to be with him, so I knew that it could not be avoided.

It was difficult to even think of leaving, because my children were very much attached to my family and I had just lost my grandfather, whom I loved very, very much.

The whole ordeal was frightening to me, because Denver was a thousand miles away from home. I asked the Lord for guidance, because I had no idea how I would deal with it. The fear never subsided, but the day came and I moved to Denver with the children.

I made the move because I was willing to do whatever it took to keep the family together. My husband was the head of the family, so I had to follow him in what he saw as right for our family.

The children and I made the move to Denver a few days before Thanksgiving. We were living with my cousin and her husband until we got settled with Jerrold's job and a place to live.

Things felt so strange because I had always been around my parents and siblings for the holidays. Thanksgiving and Christmas were important days for the Goodwin family, but I was away from my parents, nieces, nephews, brothers and sisters, aunts and uncles and my grandparents. I kept wondering about what they were all doing and who was saying what about our move to Denver.

The girls and I missed our home deeply.

Jerrold was not homesick in the least.

We would all be sitting at the dining room table eating and everything was so quiet that it made me feel uncomfortable. It made me so homesick that I would begin to cry. I would excuse myself from the table to cry in private.

Gina Johnson

Surviving On Broken Pieces

My aunt followed me one time and told me that she understood what I was feeling, because she had the same empty, homesick feeling when she first moved away.

But her empathy and support were little comfort as the pieces of my marriage and my life continued to fall apart.

Gina Johnson

Surviving On Broken Pieces

Gina Johnson

Surviving On Broken Pieces

Chapter Five: Things Fall Apart

"No matter how prosperous a man was, if he was unable to rule his women and his children, he was not really a man.//Okonkwo ruled his household with a heavy hand//Do what you are told, woman." From "Things Fall Apart," by Chinua Achebe

After the first child was born, my husband started leaving me for two months at a time. He would give me the date and the time that he would leave and he would be gone to God knows where. He would call and talk to us, but we had no idea where he was.

Gina Johnson

Surviving On Broken Pieces

I began to view him as a tyrant and a ruler more than a husband and partner.

He would do things to coerce me into doing his bidding, as opposed to lovingly leading me onto the right path for our love and our life and our family.

The hardest part was when he would leave us.

I was trying to be as tolerant and as accommodating as I could, but when Jerlina started getting older—in the second and third grade--it started affecting her. She couldn't sleep and she had migraines. He would come and pick her up but I had no idea where he was living or whether he was cheating on me.

I didn't push him to tell me, because I felt that he was already on the edge of never coming back, but over time, it was wearing me down—mostly because of how it was affecting our daughters.

He wouldn't just leave for a while to clear his head, he would move away and then move back. He would come home for six months and then leave for four. Then, he'd switch it up and come home for four months and then leave for six.

Surviving On Broken Pieces

He would run as a solution to any difficulty. Whether it was finances or me getting on his nerves, he would run.

I tried to understand his need to run, but when I would try to talk to him, I wouldn't get any real answers.

I asked him about the source of our problems and ultimately, he felt it was because of my closeness to my family. I don't know if that meant that he was jealous of my closeness to them, or if he just thought that I was too close to them in general. Either way, it made no sense.

But I would try to love him more to get him to be happy and to get him to stay.

Gina Johnson

Surviving On Broken Pieces

But it was hard to keep a love together with someone who would be so inconsistent that no real plans could be made.

For example, he was supposed to be a man of God, but he would straddle the fence in church. He would follow the rules of the church whenever he wanted to and then stop following them whenever he decided to.

I would get ready to go to church and he would be washing the car with a cigar in his mouth. Smoking was against the rules of the church. He would also be drinking and that was a major issue.

Gina Johnson

Surviving On Broken Pieces

He didn't do these things all the time, but he would do them whenever he felt like it and that was a major issue for me because I never knew that side of life. My parents didn't drink or smoke. I didn't see people in the church do those things. But my husband did them.

Jerrold was an ordained elder who drank and smoked when things got tough.

We were in the same denomination, even though we grew up in different churches.

I don't know what they did in his church, but in mine, they didn't even curse.

But he cursed.

Gina Johnson

Surviving On Broken Pieces

Jerrold cursed at me one time and it turned out to be a horrible experience. I cried for days because it hurt my feelings so deeply. He saw the impact that it had on me and he never did that again.

But I was still watching my marriage and my very self being broken into a thousand tiny pieces.

I realized that the pieces started chipping and coming apart well before they were broken.

Perhaps the breaking started because he was disappointed over not having a boy. After we had the first daughter, he asked to have another baby, and was upset that

Surviving On Broken Pieces

it wasn't a boy. He threatened to go to another woman to have a son, which is why I didn't have another child. It was just too stressful.

He loved his girls and was proud of them, but he wanted a boy. I would have had a third one, but he kept leaving, so I couldn't make it make sense.

Perhaps the breaking began with the lie about his age before we got married.

Wherever the breaking began, it was real and strong and the pieces began to fall apart.

Gina Johnson

Surviving On Broken Pieces

I hung on as long as I could, but when it affected my children, I knew I had to do something.

The last time he walked out, I couldn't take it anymore.

His mental abuse was even present in the church.

Once we were married, we were going to church together. But eventually, he started going to other churches. And those churches were of a variety of denominations—Baptist, Methodist, whatever. I think he just wanted to be a part of them so that he could attend without being seen.

Gina Johnson

Surviving On Broken Pieces

But he apparently also wanted to be able to tell lies about me to people he thought would never meet me.

He went to a well known Baptist church and I showed up. When he saw me, he shifted the speaking to someone else. The pastor and the elders met me and they were surprised that the lies he had told them about me weren't true.

People who learned after that I had difficulties with Jerrold, immediately assumed that he was beating me, but he never did. It was more of a mental abuse and emotional abuse.

Gina Johnson

Surviving On Broken Pieces

His penchant for leaving was abusive, but eventually, he turned into an angry man.

I knew that it was time to leave when became angrier and angrier.

For example, I couldn't do anything in the church, because he would become jealous.

In Denver, the pastor asked me to speak and I had a massive argument with Jerrold about it. He didn't want me to do it, but when the church found out I was a good speaker, they really wanted me to do it. He even stopped going to the church. But when they found out I was a good speaker, he stopped going.

Gina Johnson

Surviving On Broken Pieces

As a result of his jealousy, he moved from Denver abruptly.

I moved to Denver to try to save the marriage, but then, he moved away from the family without any real notice.

We moved all the way to Denver to be with him, but even that wasn't good enough for him.

One day, he just jumped up and moved us back home.

I had done everything I could to hold our marriage together, but this was the last straw. I just couldn't take his leaving anymore. I especially couldn't handle the fact that his leaving was now affecting our children in a way I couldn't ignore.

My oldest daughter used to tell me that she would pray that we would go our separate ways.

I never talked bad about him in front of the children, but they could see that things weren't good and they formed their own opinions.

My oldest daughter, Jerlina, accepted that we weren't good together and she made her peace with it. But my youngest, Dominique, had some issues. He promised her that he would never leave. But he did leave. And when he was leaving to move out of the house, he just said: "Daddy gotta do what Daddy gotta do." She was at the door crying, telling him that he had promised he wouldn't leave, but it didn't make a difference.

Jerlina was old enough to process what was occurring and she simply learned to accept it. She once told me: "I've learned to love my daddy where he is at. I don't expect things from him. He can give only what he can give and I love him right there."

My daughter accepted it, and for the first time, I accepted it as well. In my mind, I finally accepted that we weren't going to make it.

Gina Johnson

Surviving On Broken Pieces

I began to prepare myself and my daughters for life without Daddy. I would send them every summer whether they wanted to go or not.

Initially, I told him that he could come back. He didn't want to and he told me he wasn't coming back.

He thought I couldn't survive without him and he would tell me that all the time. He told me that I would lose the house, but I still have it to this day.

I only wanted him to do the right thing by our kids, especially because they were in private schools.

Gina Johnson

Surviving On Broken Pieces

I took him to court for child support because he kept leaving and I wanted him to still take care of his family. My father wouldn't allow me to divorce him. His lawyer kept telling us to get a divorce and he finally ended up filing. His lawyer didn't want any part of the divorce and eventually quit on him. His lawyer made a pass at me and admitted to the judge that he did it and stated that he needed to be recused from the case.

I spent a lot of time trying to fight for the marriage and praying: "Oh, Lord, not my marriage."

But finally, after Jerrold moved away, I said: "Lord, whatever your will is, I accept it." After that, the divorce was final one week later.

Things had finally fallen apart.

Surviving On Broken Pieces

Gina Johnson

Chapter Six: Power of A Prayerful Wife

"Lord, I pray that my husband will be strong in the Lord and put on the whole armor of God, so he can stand against the enemy every day. Enable him to take up the shield of faith, helmet of salvation, and the sword of the Spirit, which is the Word of God."--from The Power of A Praying Wife, by Stormie Omartian

I grew up in the church, so I was a prayerful woman.

And when I got married, I became a prayerful wife.

Surviving On Broken Pieces

Praying was something I was strong in, so I did it and I did it well. I did a lot of it. But I felt that God wasn't answering and didn't hear me.

I didn't think it was fair for God not to hear my prayers. I felt like I had given God my life—drinking, smoking and staying out all hours of the night--these things were foreign to me.

However, my husband would do all of those things and more. Perhaps God wasn't hearing me because I was connected to Jerrold.

I began to question God, even though I stayed true to him. When my friends

Surviving On Broken Pieces

were going a different way, I stayed with God. I didn't understand how he could allow me to go through such turmoil. I felt like he had forsaken me.

I kept my faith in him because the bible says that he will never leave you or forsake you. And, he took care of me when I couldn't take care of myself.

I was falling into a thousand pieces, but God kept me from completely falling apart.

I survived on broken pieces because God held the pieces together.

But not without the pain of breaking.

Gina Johnson

Surviving On Broken Pieces

I was breaking and I was torn up inside. I worried so much that I lost a lot of weight. I went down to a size three. I would go to church and people would look at me strangely. Due to the weight loss, I looked like a crackhead even though I had never been on crack.

The breaking was showing on my body, but I tried to hide how it was breaking on the inside.

I was trying to hide how I felt from my family when we went to church. I tried to keep the tears back. My dad would come to get me and it would be just me and my girls.

Gina Johnson

Surviving On Broken Pieces

It was easy to hide it while I was living in Denver, but once I moved back home, I knew things were visible to my family.

I lived in Denver for four years and he moved me in one week—he told me one day that we were moving and we moved that week. He sent his brother with me to move back home and to this day I don't know what it was he was trying to keep from me.

When we moved from Denver, he uprooted me without anything. No truck nothing. We had a short window of time and he just had us move what we could. He moved me and all he said is: "we are moving."

Gina Johnson

Surviving On Broken Pieces

I had to go back to the house after it sold. He gave me power of attorney and he sent his brother back to help me move. All we took were whatever clothes we could put in the suitcase and he left everything else in the realtor's hands.

When we moved back from Denver, his job transferred to Iowa and he just stopped where his job was and never came home with us. He stopped two hours away from where we grew up. He didn't move back to the city of Matteson because he had to work. He stayed down near his job at Southwest Bell and eventually, they moved him to Iowa. It was two hours away.

Gina Johnson

Surviving On Broken Pieces

I moved in with my parents and he would come every two weeks to see the kids.

When the house in Denver sold, he didn't even want to go back to sign the papers. His older brother and I packed the truck and moved it back to Matteson.

He never went back. Whatever his reason was, something was about to hit home and he didn't want it to sit on our doorstep.

I never had people calling me to say they saw him. Just strange behaviors.

Gina Johnson

Surviving On Broken Pieces

He moved to Texas after our divorce was final, but he had come to stay in Chicago briefly.

He had opened a BBQ stand. My dad had loaned him the money. He closed the business and when we were going through the divorce, he had his mother invest in a bigger location. He got it but it didn't last.

That is the only time I had ever seen another woman. I dropped my kids off at the restaurant and she introduced herself. She said she had no idea that he was married. That night he called and left a message on my phone, cursing me out. It was all over anyway and that was the only time I saw anyone else.

By that time, it was only about the kids. After a funeral, I was dropping them off. She complimented me and said that she was shocked at what she saw, because while she had expected something negative, she actually saw a good person. She was nice to me and I was nice in return.

Jerrold had told her some strange things about me.

And he had done some strange things that I couldn't understand.

He regrets it now, many wives later.
Gina Johnson

Surviving On Broken Pieces

I regret some of what happened, but many things I feel good about.

For example, I feel good about mending the relationship with his family.

His mom was a very sweet lady and she wasn't supporting what he was doing to me. I was close to her, even though for a while, I had pulled away from her.

His mother is a church going lady and she eventually cut off all contact with me so that she could remain neutral.

My parents were very active in my life so I didn't need baby sitters. They loved spending time with their grandchildren. His mother wanted to see them and I

Surviving On Broken Pieces

would let them, but they were closer to my parents.

When things were going toward divorce, relationships were strained for a while. A year after the divorce, her daughter said her mother was down about it and wanted to talk to me. She was turning sixty and they were taking her on a weekend trip. They wanted me to go and surprise her. At first I said no, but my sisters-in-law convinced me.

I got along with the whole family and the divorce and the strain hurt me as well as it hurt them because I was so close to the family. The pulling away had to come in order for me to heal.

Gina Johnson

Surviving On Broken Pieces

Pulling back to them was part of the healing process.

While I was healing, I was trying to hide how I felt from my family when we went to church. I tried to keep the tears back.

Before the woman I saw at the restaurant, I had never dealt with another woman visibly. And I never had a woman call my phone, but I was always sure there was someone else since he kept leaving. In my mind, I didn't want to think it and I kept telling myself that he just needed some space. I couldn't really accuse him of cheating because it never hit home, but he was gone for months at a time.

Gina Johnson

Surviving On Broken Pieces

I'm not stupid, so I know there was something that made him run.

I cried many nights because I didn't understand.

Eventually, I couldn't keep it all to myself. I needed to talk to someone about what I was going through. I needed to talk to someone I could trust, so I went to my father on earth.

I went to my dad and told him that I felt God had forsaken me. He said to me: "Who are you that God can't allow the devil to test and try you? Who are you that you can't go through trials and tribulations?"

Gina Johnson

Surviving On Broken Pieces

He made so much sense to me. I already understood that God would allow his children to be tested, but while I was going through my own test, I couldn't really see clearly. But after hearing the stern words from my father, I began to understand.

And I began to heal.

As the healing process came, I began to thank God for the trials and tribulations. I started realizing that I can't help anyone if I haven't gone through anything.

I suffered long because I tried to fix things instead of leaving. I tried to keep living with the broken pieces until I saw my children beginning to break.

But I didn't just give up on my marriage.

I prayed Jerrold back several times. I prayed all the time. I was teaching a young women's marriage class, so I was trying to be an example to them.

My brother Edward had been pasturing for a year and he put me over that class. My marriage was okay that first year and then it started crumbling.

My brother had confidence in me. He also had confidence in Jerrold. He had so much confidence in my husband that he wanted to make him assistant pastor, but my husband took it wrong. He said: "I ain't nobody's flunky."

Everyone around me thought that I had my relationship with God and my walk all together, but I didn't.

I grew up in the church. I knew how to sing and I knew how to shout and praise God, but until I got in trouble with my marriage and needed to pray, I really didn't know much about prayer.

Prayer had just kind of been there for most of my life. I never had to do anything, I just prayed while everyone else was praying. I felt God's love, but I never really had to call on that love for myself until my marriage fell apart.

At first, I began praying at the church alone. I started timing myself—first, five minutes, even though it would seem like two hours.

I felt awkward, stupid and foolish.

I had grown up around prayer warriors, so praying myself should have been no problem.

But I didn't really have a prayer life. I began to get a prayer life through what I was going through. I knew how to sing and how to behave in service, but I didn't really know God for who he was. When things got bad, I could quote the scripture, but I couldn't really locate the scripture in the Bible. But I knew it was in there.

I kept praying until it came to me.

I began to tap into the realness and I began to cry out.

Sometimes, the stress was so bad that I felt like my mind was going to pop.

I'm a supervisor of women in the church's jurisdiction. I wouldn't have been able to get there without being tested.

I was tested and I prayed.

Gina Johnson

Surviving On Broken Pieces

Once I initiated a real relationship with God, God began to speak to me and deal with me.

God began to deal with Gina.

And I began to realize that while this had begun because of Jerrold's actions, that it really wasn't about Jerrold.

It was about me connecting with God.

I prayed for one year—day and after day, at my church alone.

God was doing something inside of me.

I had allowed the devil to make me angry, bitter and unforgiving, thinking it

Surviving On Broken Pieces

was all about Jerrold, but it was all about me.

I laid on the altar and cried out to God not wanting to let go of my demons, instead, wanting to focus on Jerrold.

My prayers became focused: "God, your will be done!"

The more I prayed, the more God dealt with Gina.

And without really noticing the transition, I acquired a prayer life of my own.

I could share this prayer life with others. Like my Dad, who has an awesome

Surviving On Broken Pieces

prayer life. I began to go at least one day a week with him to his home to pray.

I remember being at home alone and feeling lonely, unwanted and rejected.

I felt a great deal of pressure—like I was going to break.

I heard the voice of the Lord, saying: "I will never leave you or forsake you."

And I knew what I needed to do.

I was powerful in my prayer. First, I prayed for the marriage. And when I realized that the marriage may not be salvageable, I began to pray for healing.

Gina Johnson

Surviving On Broken Pieces

I prayed for myself and for my daughters, but I also prayed for Jerrold, because I was a family person.

I begged God to promise me that he wouldn't allow Jerrold to be lost. Despite what he had done to me, I still loved him, and I just didn't want him to be lost.

He was my first and only, and for a long time, even while I was healing, I thought that I would never get married or fall in love again.

But I had to make a break.

I called Jerrold and asked him to forgive me.

Gina Johnson

Surviving On Broken Pieces

And then I forgave him.

In a marriage, when there is a downfall, it is never on one person. Each person must be responsible for their portion, whether it is twenty-five per cent or fifty per cent.

Sometimes, as church people, we fail to see our own wrong doing. But through prayer, I began to see where I was wrong and what I needed to do to make adjustments.

I knew I had to get rid of the bitterness, the anger and the feeling that all is lost.

With God on my side, I knew I could fight the devil properly. I could fight the feelings of depression and rejection.
Gina Johnson

Surviving On Broken Pieces

I knew I had cried my last tears over my marriage and over Jerrold.

It was time for restoration.

My hope had returned while my brokenness was exiting.

My faith would lead me into restored confidence and restored ability to believe in all things good, because all things can be good through God.

Prayer works and prayer is powerful, but faith without work is dead.

In order for prayer to be the most effective in our lives, we must strengthen our faith and strengthen our selves.

Gina Johnson

Surviving On Broken Pieces

And our strength comes even through the greatest of tests.

Surviving On Broken Pieces

Gina Johnson

Chapter Seven: The Test of the Devil

"It is written: 'Man shall not live on bread alone, but on every word that comes from the mouth of God.' Jesus said to him, "Away from me, Satan! For it is written: 'Worship the Lord your God, and serve him only. Then the devil left him, and angels came and attended him." -- Matthew 4, VI-II

I was in a very good place.

I had come to understand why I had fallen apart in the first place.

Surviving On Broken Pieces

I knew that without God as an anchor, I couldn't keep the pieces from falling apart.

I also knew that the task at hand was to sweep up all the broken pieces, so that I could learn to live on the new pieces of me that were emerging.

But first, I had to finish my fight with the devil.

While I was working on my relationship with God and working on my mental health, the devil was working on other areas of my life.

He began with my finances.

Gina Johnson

Surviving On Broken Pieces

Without Jerrold supporting the family, I was losing everything around me.

I was losing my home, I couldn't afford my children's private school, I couldn't put gas in the car and I couldn't put an offering in the plate on Sunday.

It was making me weary. I was tired of leaning on mommy/daddy/sister/brother.

The first thing I changed was my attitude. I told myself that I would never be broke again.

I also told myself that through God, there would be abundance.

Gina Johnson

Surviving On Broken Pieces

I was able to save my home. I went to court with God as my focus and things just worked themselves out.

I had a brand new car that I got just before the divorce. I couldn't even afford to put gas in it. I remember going to the gas station with five dollars in coins.

I remember God speaking to me, telling me to never say that I was broke again. As a symbol, I bought a gold coin and kept it with me. No matter how low my finds got, I kept that gold coin with me as a reminder that I wasn't broke-- because I had the coin.

Gina Johnson

Surviving On Broken Pieces

The devil was testing me with my children as well.

My children were looking at me to be their rock and I had to be that for them. We had help from my family, but those girls still needed their daddy.

Jerrold and I had shared custody, so they would go with him for the summer and while they were with him, I would pray for them. I would pray for their relationship with their father, because I knew they needed him. They needed to be able to love him.

I asked God to give me wisdom with my girls. I came to understand that their relationship with him was separate from what I had known with him. My job as their mother was to nurture their relationship with him, so I would tell them to love and respect him no matter what.

They were able to keep things in perspective because they loved God.

I would sit with them and have long talks about love and forgiveness and how, through God, they had to love and forgive their father. I told them that no matter what they thought about their father's relationship with me, that it had nothing to do with them.

Gina Johnson

Surviving On Broken Pieces

My children are grown now.

They are healthy and well adjusted with their own relationships with their father.

They came through better than I had imagined, because I allowed them to deal with things in the ways that made sense for them.

They were discovering who they were and I allowed them to, helping them to keep everything in perspective.

I had to rediscover who I was in order to become what I am.

I had to look at who I was in order to heal the broken pieces.

Gina Johnson

Surviving On Broken Pieces

Gina Johnson

Chapter Eight: Who Am I?

"The most painful thing is losing yourself in the process of loving someone too much, and forgetting that you are special too." Ernest Hemingway

Sometimes, you lose in love. You lose the one person you thought was going to be there for you, no matter what.

And when you lose that person, you lose other things. You lose the bond of family that you had with your spouse and with your children. You lose houses, cars and other material possessions.

Surviving On Broken Pieces

But the greatest loss is when you lose yourself.

I lost myself in the marriage with Jerrold.

I felt alone and even though I wanted to save the marriage, I felt like nothing I could possibly do was good enough. His mind was geared to what he wanted and he couldn't hear anything I said. No matter how hard I tried and prayed, he was determined to ruin everything that we had built inside of the marriage.

My parents have been married nearly sixty years, so it was hard for me to deal with the fact that I was failing in such a short time. I had to accept the fact that this man just didn't want to be with me.

When you realize that the person you love doesn't love you, you have to accept it and create a plan to move on with your life.

Jerrold no longer loved me and I had to accept it and move on. There was no getting around it--that was the bottom line.

And it was difficult for me, because I had built my entire world around him.

My idea of family was based on what we had created. And I was certain that I would have that family with him.

Gina Johnson

Surviving On Broken Pieces

My idea of marriage was based on what we had. And even when things began to get difficult, I was still certain that we would work things out and stay married-- literally until death do us part. But I had to accept that we had divergent concepts of marriage.

My idea of who I was as a wife, a member of the family we had created, was based on something that was now changing.

Everything was changing.

Realizing that the marriage was ending forced me to accept that things were changing in many ways.

Gina Johnson

Surviving On Broken Pieces

I was changing in many ways.

I was changing so much that I wasn't certain who I really was.

It wasn't just that I didn't know who I was it was more or less that I had to find out who I was becoming, because I no longer knew who I was.

My marriage was changing. My life was changing. And I was changing.

It was time for me to find me.

I was on a search to find out who I would have to be in order to balance my life out. I had to find out what would make sense for me, so that I could move

Surviving On Broken Pieces

forward beyond this dark period in my life and find the light again.

If it were just me, I probably could have weathered whatever storm might have been coming. I probably could have stayed in the darkness and wallowed in the confusion, pain and anguish that were threatening to take over my life.

But I had two people who depended on me being stable and present. My children needed me to find myself so that they could have something to hold on to.

So I had to find myself.

Nearly every day, I was asking myself: "Who am I?"

Gina Johnson

Surviving On Broken Pieces

In answering that question, a big part of it was the grounding that I had as a child.

I went back to the center of everything.

I knew that my foundation was church. I was grounded in the Lord, but where do you go when you feel like everything has failed you?

I think for a minute, I tried to be okay with the fact that my husband was at least still in the house, which meant that we looked good on the outside.

But on the inside, I was a mess.

Gina Johnson

Surviving On Broken Pieces

I didn't even know that I was depressed. I was taught that depression is of the devil.

But I was also taught that God is hope, even though it took me a moment to get to the point where I could embrace that hope.

In the meantime, I continued to fall apart.

And it began to show on the outside as well.

I began losing weight and falling deeper away from myself.

Gina Johnson

Surviving On Broken Pieces

I tried to hold on to the lessons from childhood.

My mom used to always say that no matter what happens, you don't let anyone take you away from who you are.

But I had been moved away from who I was so slowly, that by the time I looked up, too much of me was already gone. The loving person was gone and the smiles were gone. I'm normally a happy person, but the happiness was gone and the smiles weren't real anymore. I was smiling on the outside, but messed up on the inside.

Gina Johnson

Surviving On Broken Pieces

Jerrold didn't want to be there and it got to the point, where I didn't want him to be there, but because of the way I was raised, I couldn't bring myself to express how I was feeling inside, because I wasn't supposed to feel that way.

Even in church--I was crying on the inside until I realized where my hope was.

My hope was in Christ.

The failing marriage had me unhappy, but deep down inside, it couldn't mess with my joy, because my joy was not just in me, it was in Christ.

Gina Johnson

Surviving On Broken Pieces

Since my joy was centered in Christ, happiness was my destination. My joy came from God, so it couldn't be destroyed and it couldn't waiver.

It took a moment to get to that realization, but once I got there, things began to make sense.

After the divorce, I went into a thing. I was confused, but I felt that I could be happy again.

I felt that I could be happy without my husband, even though I was unhappy with him. It was turmoil in my mind.

Gina Johnson

Surviving On Broken Pieces

I was thirty-eight when I got divorced. And initially, I thought that was it for me.

I didn't believe in divorce, but I realize that things happen for a reason and I had to move beyond it.

I began to quote scripture.

I quoted scripture to myself without referring to the Bible to find what I needed. Even if I couldn't find it, I could quote it, because it had always been inside of me.

I had to speak to myself and say out loud: "I'm a child of God. God loves me." Speaking my truth helped to get me

Gina Johnson

through the darkness, instead of dwelling in the feeling that there was no love.

I knew God was there even though, for a moment, I didn't feel it. I knew it.

I began to quote scripture to myself regularly and frequently.

I'd get in the hot tub and I would literally feel my mind pop from the pressure. But I knew how to get to the word.

I would quote scripture to myself and then talk to God. I would say: "God you promised to keep my mind at perfect peace and I belong to you. I know this is

Surviving On Broken Pieces

a problem you allowed to happen, so you can fix it."

I was taught that you fight the devil with God's word.

But I also had to learn that not everyone that claimed to be was truly focused on God's word.

I went to a Christian psychologist. After the first session, he asked me to bring a picture of my husband.

He put the picture on the board and told me to repeat after him: "I love his dirty drawers."

Gina Johnson

Surviving On Broken Pieces

I didn't repeat it and I stopped going after that.

What help was that? I shouldn't have been in there. My trust was in God. God was trying to bring me to the place where I needed to be, but I was going to places of confusion.

Then I went to a medical doctor, because I couldn't sleep at night. The doctor put me on pills for depression. I took one and it took me to where I thought I was nuts. I was just sitting around crying like I was losing my mind.

My dad sent my brother Reuben to come and get the pills and flush them down

Surviving On Broken Pieces

the toilet. Reuben called my dad and said: "I took care of the problem."

Again, God was telling me what I needed to hear. I just needed to listen.

And I knew I couldn't be depressed, because that was of the devil.

And I knew that I had to find my way out of that dark, cold place because of my children.

My daughters were my reason to keep pushing and to keep trying. But for a moment, when you're that down, even though you try to keep it from them you really can't. I tried to hide it but kids are smart—smarter than we think.

Gina Johnson

Surviving On Broken Pieces

They knew that things were different and that things weren't very good.

At that point, there could be no more darkness, I had them to hold on to. I had to finish raising them.

That's when I began to get it back together.

I knew I was a mother.

I knew I was a child of God.

I knew who I was raised to be.

And I knew that I was going to be alright as long as I returned to the things that would never change.

Gina Johnson

Surviving On Broken Pieces

Gina Johnson

Chapter Nine: Putting All The Pieces Back Together Again

"God, pick up the pieces of my life. Put me back together again. I give you my praise." Jeremiah 17, v 14

When we are broken, we search for healing wherever we think we can find it.

But I believe that there is only healing in God.

I don't believe that there is true healing in the medication that the doctors prescribe or in the psychoanalysis that we seek from the psychiatrists. I sought out that kind of healing and it didn't work. And my family knew it wasn't going to work, so they literally came to me and took me away from it and took it away from me.

In addition to believing that only God can heal me, I also believe that God is the only complete healing.

I know that some people can find comfort in medication (not healing, but comfort), and that some healing can even come from talking to professional counselors. But neither of those methods can offer complete healing.

Gina Johnson

Surviving On Broken Pieces

Complete healing can only come from a heartfelt relationship with God

God's children know the story of Job in the Bible.

We know that Job went through many, many trials and tribulations in his life. We know that Job lost everything, including his worldly possessions and his children. He even lost his faith in God. But the trials he went through moved him closer to God. And in moving closer to God, Job found the faithfulness of God.

Now, I won't compare myself to Job, because although I lost a great deal and I

Surviving On Broken Pieces

was truly tested, I didn't lose it all. I still have my children, my family and my health.

I was broken, but I believe that I was able to keep from losing the pieces of myself because I turned to God before things went too far to be retrieved.

Sometimes, when you don't know what to do and you feel that all is lost, prayer and reading the word is key. You have to stay around the people of God. They will have good messages for you. If the devil can get you alone and get you depressed, he will win. Stay with those who are in the spirit.

Gina Johnson

Surviving On Broken Pieces

Sometimes, you will break down.

As women, sometimes, we think that it's okay to cry and okay to fall apart and stay there.

It's always okay to cry, but it's never okay to quit. We must endure.

I want women to know that they can survive.

Sometimes women get broken and they stay broken.

In addition to God's armor, it's okay to use some of the armor of the world that women have always used.

Gina Johnson

Surviving On Broken Pieces

Look at yourself in the mirror and love yourself. Dress yourself up and acknowledge to the world that you are beautifully made by God.

Put on that dress and heels.

Empower yourself with some of the world, but let nothing hinder you from your walk with the Lord.

Even if you don't know where the scripture is found, you will know where the word is in you.

It will come alive within you.

It came alive in me.

Gina Johnson

Surviving On Broken Pieces

It was about the strength coming out of me. I had to get to know my own strength. If you never go through anything, you can't help anyone.

You can't take my glory, if you can't take my story.

And my blessings came to me and began to multiply.

After saying I would never love again and never marry again, in 2009, I remarried. I met and fell in love with Phillip Johnson. Sr., whom God sent to me and who has loved me for who I am. He has embraced my love for God and for the church.

Forgiveness is a big key.
    Gina Johnson

Surviving On Broken Pieces

I forgave Jerrold, and in doing so, I forgave myself for participating and allowing the brokenness to occur.

And because God helped me to forgive Jerrold, I'm to have cordial conversations with him. We can attend events with the children and be cool with each other.

God forgives us, so our duty is to forgive others and to forgive ourselves.

God made me strong enough to survive on my broken pieces.

He helped me to survive and to reassemble to broken pieces and he changed me.

Gina Johnson

Surviving On Broken Pieces

He changed my finances and he changed my heart. He let me understand the you don't have to be bitter and upset because prayer changes things.

Surviving on broken pieces didn't change my situation, but it changed me so that the situation could change.

Sometimes the situation doesn't change, but if you're sincere about your walk with God, he can change you.

Where my life was severely broken, it is now whole.

I have a daughter in her second year of law school.

Gina Johnson

Surviving On Broken Pieces

I have another who gave me two beautiful grandchildren with my son-in-law.

My new husband has four children, so now I have sons that I never had. The youngest son was three when we got married.

I still drive the Lexus that I struggled to put gas in.

My children stayed in the private schools until graduation.

The post dated checks that I wrote to the church-I paid every one of them.

Gina Johnson

Surviving On Broken Pieces

At 49, I became the jurisdictional supervisor of women in the church. Typically, women are much older when that happens.

I found love again. I have a really good husband who moved me to bigger and better things in life.

My finances are better than they've ever been.

I'm not bitter about anything I've gone through because I've worked through it all.

Once I got beyond bitterness, I knew it was time to share my story.

Gina Johnson

Surviving On Broken Pieces

Gina Johnson

Chapter Ten: Sharing My Story

"Therefore do not be ashamed of the testimony about our Lord, nor of me his prisoner, but share in suffering for the gospel by the power of God,⁹ who saved us and called us to a holy calling, not because of our works but because of his own purpose and grace, which he gave us in Christ Jesus before the ages began." 2 Timothy, 1, v 8-9

They say that the best way for God to heal a person is to give him all the broken pieces.

Gina Johnson

Surviving On Broken Pieces

I presented my broken pieces to God.

Giving the broken pieces to God means that we have to be honest with God and lay everything out.

But first, we have to be honest with ourselves.

I believe I was honest in laying out the ways in which I was broken and identifying all of the little pieces. And because I was honest with myself, I was able to be honest with God.

I had laid everything out for myself. Laying it all out for God required some divine inspiration.

Gina Johnson

Surviving On Broken Pieces

I found my inspiration at a church service. It seemed as though the pastor was preaching directly to me. That was the start of me restoring myself by beginning to write.

I remember it like it was today. We had an Easter revival at our church. I was struggling within myself to go. I was feeling down and somewhat defeated, but I got the strength within myself to go to the revival.

I sat there trying to fight back the tears. Life was hitting me from every angle—my finances, my children, my self esteem and my so-called friends. It

Surviving On Broken Pieces

seemed like my world was turning for the worst.

I got in the church and sat in my seat fighting the tears. It was time for the preacher to preach. His name was Pastor Hutton. He began to read the scripture and he said: "Tonight's message is about surviving on broken pieces." And he preached the heck out of it.

Pastor Hutton was preaching and tears began to flow heavy as I sat there and said to myself: "That's me. I'm broken, but I can survive this."

I left that service that night knowing that what I was going through was not going

Surviving On Broken Pieces

to be death. I was still alive and still vital. My pieces may have been broken, but I was a survivor.

I went home and began to write my story.

I was surviving on broken pieces and part of putting them back together was telling my story.

God said: "W rite."

So I began to write.

I wrote when I was broken and I wrote as I began to heal.

I was broken.

Gina Johnson

Surviving On Broken Pieces

And when you're broken, sometimes you think that it's all about your own brokenness, but really, God is setting you up to be a messenger after your triumph.

As I went through the life changing experience of my pieces being broken, I realized that it wasn't about me or Jerold, but in fact, God was trying to do something with me. God was trying to take me somewhere I needed to be.

God was setting me up to be used for others, to help them through their test.

As I came out on the other side, I understood that my writing was about more than just getting my story on paper.

Gina Johnson

Surviving On Broken Pieces

It was about sharing my story to empower other people.

People are broken every day.

Young women have been damaged but there's a healing process you go through to put the pieces back together. God can put the pieces back together if you let him work in you.

Just because you've been in the church all your life doesn't mean that the puzzle is complete. You may be looking at portions of the puzzle, so the portions look complete.

Gina Johnson

Surviving On Broken Pieces

Sometimes, the puzzle has to be broken in order for the pieces to make sense as a whole.

And, so my writing—this book—is for people who have been tested, or people who are in the middle of their tests.

This book is for the person who may have been molested by her father and is feeling that God has forsaken her and is not concerned.

People can be broken from sexual abuse.

God is able to heal all of that.

There are women around the world who have gone through things and the pieces

Surviving On Broken Pieces

in their life may be broken. This book is for them.

This book may touch the lives of people on drugs. They may be battling the demons of drug abuse and in need of a message. I hope this book can inspire them to heal.

I hope my story of surviving on broken pieces can help someone else battling through the difficulty of torn relationships and broken marriages.

This story is to let you know that God can always take those broken pieces and put them back together again.

Gina Johnson

Surviving On Broken Pieces

No matter where your brokenness may be, God is able to put it back together. He will put it back together so well, people won't even see the scars.

Where the devil tried to destroy my mind, my mind is now at peace.

And, why wouldn't the devil come after me and try to destroy me? The devil tried to destroy the greatest soldier of God—Jesus himself—and through the love of God, the faithfulness to God, Jesus was victorious and so was I.

As humans, our flesh is naturally weak. The body itself can only take so much. The heart and mind can only take so much before breaking and being destroyed. But God gives us armor that shores us up and protects us as we fight the battles of life. With that armor, we can always win.

"Be strong in the Lord and in his mighty power. Put on the full armor of God, so that you can take your stand against the devil's schemes. For our struggle is not against flesh and blood, but against the spiritual forces of evil. Therefore put on the full armor of God, so that you may be able to stand your ground. Stand firm then, with the belt of truth buckled around your waist, with the breastplate of righteousness in place. In addition to all this, take up the shield of faith, with which you can extinguish

all the flaming arrows of the evil one. Take the helmet of salvation and the sword of the Spirit, which is the word of God." Ephesians 6:10-17

We take up the armor because we are too weak alone in our own flesh to fight the battles that will surely come to us.

Those battles will come to us because there is no great and good life without having been tested by the devil, knowing that you have been baptized by the fire.

No matter what your challenge, you can overcome it, but you must be tested in order to appreciate the blessings, which will come after the testing is done.

Gina Johnson

Surviving On Broken Pieces

We learn in Corinthians that God will not allow us to be tested beyond what we can survive.

"No testing has overtaken you except what is common to mankind. And God is faithful; he will not let you be tested beyond what you can bear. But when you are tested; he will also provide a way out so that you can endure it." 1 Corinthians, 10:13

I was tested.

And I was broken.

And I'm here to tell you that I survived.

And, I want people to know that they can survive the storms of life. With the

Surviving On Broken Pieces

help of the Lord and by putting God first--no matter what, you WILL be able to conquer and not just come out of it, but come out of top with more than what you had when you went into it.

You WILL be able to survive.

And, you will be able to survive on broken pieces.

Gina Johnson